21st Century Autoimmune Blues

21st Century Autoimmune Blues

Brent Terry

21st Century Autoimmune Blues
Copyright © 2021 Brent Terry
All Rights Reserved
Published by Unsolicited Press
Printed in the United States of America.
First Edition.

No part of this book may be used or reproduced in any manner whatsoever without written permission except in the case of brief quotations embodied in critical articles or reviews.

Attention schools and businesses: for discounted copies on large orders, please contact the publisher directly.

For information contact:
Unsolicited Press
Portland, Oregon
www.unsolicitedpress.com
orders@unsolicitedpress.com
619-354-8005

Cover Design: Kathryn Gerhardt
Editor: S.R. Stewart

ISBN: 978-1-950730-96-4

For Terry

I would like to thank the following fine journals for publishing some of the poems found in this book:

Spillway Magazine: "Ashbery Before Bedtime"

The RiseUp Review: "They Told Me I Couldn't Write about Birds and Flowers Anymore, What with all the Injustice in the World" and "My Meme"

Turnip Truck(s): "The End of Wonder?"

The Undertow Review: "After the Burning Bush, the First Firefly of Summer" and "Black is the New Black" (from "Monochrome Attic")

Rattle: "21st Century Autoimmune Blues" and "What Happens in Church"

Drunken Boat: "Mirage Hypothesis"

Adirondack Review: "Freedom Toast"

Coachella Review: "Rancid, Gladys"

Queen Mob's Teahouse: "EDM (Ecstasy Defies Me)" and "Sock Hop"

Spittoon: "The Murder in Her He(art)"

The Connecticut River Review: "The Torrent Is a Harbinger"

The Ekphrastic Review: "The Runners in the Snow" and "Nude Descending a Staircase"

Scoundrel Time: "Flotsam"

Contents

Overture   11

    My Heartthrob Dreams of Eden: Ars Poetica for Two Voices   12

Playing Tag with Gravity   17

    They Told Me I Couldn't Write about Birds and Flowers Anymore, What with all the Injustice in the World   18

    Death at the Food Truck Rodeo   20

    The End of Wonder?   22

    They've Kidnapped the Muse, Apparently   23

    After the Burning Bush, the First Firefly of Summer   26

    The Torrent Is a Harbinger   28

    Solstice   30

    In the East the Runners are Rising   32

    My Meme   34

    1972   37

    Oh Say Can You See? (The King of Space Disco Plays Camden Yards)   39

    55   41

    A Field Guide to Migratory Birds   43

    21st Century Autoimmune Blues   45

The Enchantment of Blue Bamboozles	47
Mirage Hypothesis	48
The Spraycan Picassos	50
Gusher	53
Ashbery Before Bedtime	55
Pan-Olympic	57
Asian Fusion Cuisine (Or: Takeout Meets its Match in Young Jack Spratt)	59
EDM (Ecstasy Defies Me)	61
Monochrome Attic #1	62
crimson, no clover	63
Cabin Fever (Sculpture Garden in Security Light)	65
True Bride	67
Rancid, Gladys	69
Freedom Toast	71
In Cambridge, Maybe	72
Aurora Borealis	74
The Razorteeth of Newsfeed	77
Hotel Ashbery	78
Sock Hop	83
Note to Self	85
Racial Profiling for Dummies	87
The Runners in the Snow	88

What Happens in Church	90
On Encountering a Rack of Hogwarts Panties at Target the Husband Has an Existential Crisis	92
Live Model at the Salon for Abject Expressionists	95
Nude Descending a Staircase	97
Carbon Taxing	99
God Particle	100
Flotsam	102
Coda: The Murder in Her He(art)	105
The Murder in her He(art)	106

Overture

My Heartthrob Dreams of Eden: Ars Poetica for Two Voices

(A [Whit]Manic Episode)

I am a Kosmos caught in a songbird's trill.

I speak from strands of chlorophyll.

Voodoo ventriloquist, I throw my voice

under the bus, embrace the crush,
bash my verbiage into Babel, brouhaha, birdseed for the beaks
of a million

mockingbirds.

Murder

and murmuration, I travel on the tongues
of the hungry hordes, the bleats of kids,

the honks of Fords.

I lick the flowers that foam at your mouth:
kisses tricked with tattletale taste.

I translate your face
into appleblossom, forsythia,
cherryfroth imbibed
by inebriate throngs.

My ferment fuels your drinking songs.

Push my buttons, I'm the gadget
that talks the book.

Come fish my lines for juicy hooks.

I'm the babble that tickles the throat
of the brook, the trout in the flood,
the chum in the blood.

Hammerhead that frenzies your famished brain.

I am pain alchemized to aria,
high-C held until the raincloud breaks.

I salve your aches.

I sing your rage.

I am Hendrix to your Page.

I singe the body electric, torch the axe from which your Phoenix flies.

I'm the hex that stokes your sex,
ivy that feeds your itch,
hallelujah chorus
in the temple of the body as god.

Aztec heartthrob, I sing to your sacrifice when the only way left to go

is down.

I bid you drown.
I bid you spit in the rictus of power,
nibble at the nexus of the cactus flower,

the hocus-pocus locus:
abracadabra candelabra
that fevers your demon dreams.

These visions are exactly what they seem:

Virgins caught in a pyramid scheme.

I'm their hero—their Virgil—and I'm ready to fight, all gonzo in the monkey light.

The virgins, freed, shout, 'Hell's Bells, Dude!'

Begin to rap Beatitudes.

Now we're living La Vita Nuova!

Every devil loves a Bossa Nova diva.

And aren't we all Earth's children here?
Let's chill the blood lust, grab a beer.

Captain, yo, Captain! Come jam a tune,

jazz some June,

*razz the stars to throw
some glitter down.*

God-fodder gowned in sweat and skin,
I *dig* the condition our condition is in. Sin

*is a glint in the eye of the beholder,
an answer to the body's question.*

So shimmy my ancient hippie shake,

shimmer your buds until they break.

Binge the passionflower that bleeds you out:
symphony of timpani; moonglint whispers
from obsidian blades.

Guitar gods and erstwhile virgins
ride waves of sound and heat.

I cut out my own heart, the better to dance its beat.

Playing Tag with Gravity

They Told Me I Couldn't Write about Birds and Flowers Anymore, What with all the Injustice in the World

Something there is that doesn't love a wall. —Robert Frost

In Arizona, in Texas, from desert dust it rises.
From barrel cactus and Christmas agate
it grows, from the bleached bones
of javelina, the ribcages of a mother
and twin girls from Chajul. It is Ozymandius;
it is April and the Lupine shoot their purple
arrows through the husks of cars.
Globe Mallow, Desert Senna, Mojave Spurge
and Brittlebush have their own notion
of freedom. Birdsong goes wherever
the fuck it pleases: Green Jay,
Chachalaca, Bobwhite proclaiming its name;
wintering Western Meadowlark sings
a migration song, wings its way
toward Wyoming above Tacomas loaded
with Slim Jims and zip-tied Salvadorans.
Was there a time before beauty was ironic?
When bloom was not torment, birdsong
not yet taunt? To the north the broccoli flowers,

then rots in the fields, uncut. I hope
this Bloodflower, this Primrose, this Indian
Paintbrush won't spoil the poem. This Gila
Woodpecker, this Chipa Amarillo, this Inca Dove.

Death at the Food Truck Rodeo

Oh, how like love, to be stung by the first bee
of summer! The stab, the electric thrum
that numbs your fingers, dispatches your lemonade
earthward, the burrito anointed in sweet
green chili now a part of your ensemble.
Bespattered by the divine, your EpiPen on top
of the dresser next to your cufflinks
and copy of *Howl*, your friends are still en-route,
your love in Duluth, bee still dangling
from the webbing between your forefinger
and thumb, and what you need, you think,
is to sink to your knees among the tender young tufts
between *Falafel Kingdom* and *The Burrito Bandito*,
to be floored by the hivebuzzed blossoming
of tinnitus, the shouts of children, the caffeinated
strum and brass of Mariachis, the fading chorus
of faces stuffed with dough. You are bewitched
by the shadows of leaves, hand-painted signs
for *Cubanos y Coca-Cola*, the acid-trip, eight-foot
radioactive habañero lacerating the aluminum
skin of the taco truck across the green.
It all starts to prism, to whirl, the whole panorama

bright as fruit and booze in a blender.
You try to swallow, to speak. Your lips attempt
to wrap themselves around "a bee" or "goodbye".
Here on Earth your back is caressed by green tendrils,
but you are beginning to bob, to balloon
yourself cloudward. Fluid fills your fingers
and your lungs. The sky fills with helium,
a high-pitched holy hollering. It's only love,
and thus the birds commence with their elegies
and elaborate dances. Your grandmother warbles
a tune she sang when you were just a boy.
Your lover whispers *hush*, then ghosts your lips
with kisses. Some new music, systemic as summer,
as anaphylaxis, now courses through your body
like cotton-candy or fire. You are a world. You orbit
yourself. You're so full of life you could explode
into a billion hyacinths and then you do.

The End of Wonder?

(an inauguration ode)

It was the year of weird food and devastation.
The dancehalls were torched, poets kicked apart,
verses left to bleed out in the bushes.
The victors raged their giddy flags from the backs
of pickups, ground the fleeing children
beneath their oversized tires. Mothers shamble
the barrens still, operatic effigies calling baby,
baby, please.

Bodies sing from the trees.

It never rains anymore, but when it does
the rivers devour their bridges, scour the burned
encampments, carve new nightmares into badlands
of slag and ash. Somebody says a blessing
over the tater tots. Somebody organizes the ammo.
Someone writes a hymn for the drowning,
but the singers are shitfaced in the choirloft.
Through the holes in your roof the stars come in
to kiss you in your sleep.

They've Kidnapped the Muse, Apparently

so you answer the ransom note with cereal in milk,
spill the beans about dreams of murder-
suicide pacts with imaginary friends and mother
figures you once borrowed from books. Maybe
you should shatter yourself, swallow the shards. A mosaic
goes glitterball in the gut, light by which you might

sparkle your ass on out of here. By which you might
glyph the monochrome horizon, featureless as milk.
The sky is a gallery wall. Mayhap you should hang a mosaic
of baby pics and dropped crockery, murder
your crows in a burst of blood and feathers, make, maybe,
mobiles of birdsfeet and beaks crying *mother, mother.*

You rinse out your bowl, call your mother.
She says come for the weekend. You say you might.
She says she has a friend with a daughter; *maybe....*
You want to drown yourself in milk.
You say maybe Saturday, the Friday traffic's murder.
On your ceiling passing cars make a mosaic

of refracted, reflected light. A kaleidoscope, a mosaic
that moves to the music of whoosh and hum. The mother
of all headaches blooms behind your eyes. You could murder
a burger right now, a basket of fries. You think you might
find yourself a booth in a tavern somewhere, milk
the drainpipe hours in a haze of brew and grease. Maybe

you've had too much to think—too little to drink. Maybe
you should let the chorus in your brain do their thing: mosaic
of hosannas etched on dark descending, drunk on milk
of paradise. All percussion and wail, these mother-
fuckers split you open like overripe fruit. You think you might
now be capable of art. You might now be capable of murder.

So you uncap yourself like a poison pen, bleed out in a murder
of melodies like an assassin with a jones for jazz. Maybe
you should get out more. Maybe you might
break a battalion of bottles over a squadron of heads, a mosaic
of smash blossoming like alleycats in your brain. The godmother
of refugees with bomb-strapped hearts feeds you all feral like
        milk.

There might be an angel in your Alpha-Bits, muttering about murder.

There may be a devil in your Alpha-Bits, and she's making a mosaic.

She thinks she'll call you *Glitterball with Feathers and Mother's Milk*.

After the Burning Bush, the First Firefly of Summer

I'm in no hurry, what with the lightning bug text messages,
wobbly bricks in the Willimantic sidewalk, streetlight
spilling moon or glass or fragrant *You-Know-Who* at a party.
God, be in my head, the fence ablaze; your name
doesn't matter. The years I begged to dig holes
as a way of working through you. I am proud
to share my candy corn with other kids like me.
One should have the appropriate head: orange lilies,
my co-star cast against type this time, and dangerous,
the cold, cold syllables like ripples on black water.
And then I sprang from the yellow taxi, the driver
with the checkered past fuming with a light
corrosive breath, a half-molten microwave beef
and bean burrito in the coagulated Connecticut heat.
But there is also a dark district where one may
do whatever she tells me, and don't ask questions.
Behind the barn, behind the gingerbread yurt, sex,
and the city burning astride the river. Tender ones!
You jam love on pawnshop Stratocasters.
I'll mock you until I've had enough, like a drunk
sergeant singing in bed. Not sin, but satisfaction

at first light. I would want a copy of *that* photograph!
Is this happening? Or is it a mirage of parachutes
and pretty sex, precise as brushstrokes after a six-pack.
A pomegranate. A red, red pickup truck. People say
I'm killing myself falling into my own aortal puddle,
but they can't see *You-Know-Who* and me,
the volcanic sunset, the red night clouds. One of us
dreams of water, one of us wears pajamas made of fire.

The Torrent Is a Harbinger

Garden Bridge, Willimantic, CT

Raining again, and between my window
and the pink Victorian across the river
hangs a curtain of concrete lace.
Through its folds the abandoned thread-
mills dissolve, reconstitute themselves
as lofts, as studios where, as we speak,
painters in Nirvana T-shirts and spattered
jeans shout color at canvas, cry and hue
that until this moment existed only
as rumor, delicious as whispers trickled
tongue-to-ear from one grizzled relic
to another, rocking westward
like spicetrade troubadours conjuring
the impossibility of cardamom
from pockets of silk. The river thunders
with snowmelt, the bones of ruined works
raising a havoc of current and froth.
I want to smash something until it sings.
I want to set the choirloft alight, speak
in tongues that torch the silent tabernacle
where winter kneels, worrying its beads

and murmuring. I want to sing you back,
little brother, from the dead.

Every blossom bursts from a rupturing
and from my chest these bulbs scream
your tulips out into the innocent air.
Silver hammers pound their syllables of rain
into my skull. Who knows what riot
provokes the painter's hand—deft thrust
into a puddle of alazzarin crimson,
spasm of some rare blue—the incendiary
stroke, the cinnamon whiff, vibrato
that throbs from brain
to brush, bristles igniting a furious bloom.

for Scott, In Memoriam, Easter, 2017

Solstice

She's winsome; she's lost some
momentum to the rote vocabulary
of a dying afternoon.

Bare trees fingerpick melodies
from shingles mosshung darkly
on walls of lavender light.

Empty-throated until springtime, birdhouses
sway, blocky Baryshnikovs branch-dancing,
mute in the tuneless breeze.

Teacup. Hiccup. Is this a stick-up?
She sings Tuesday's a time for tallying losses,
volleying kisses long-since puckered and gone.

She sweeps, sashays, gainsays
the caffeinated, dirty ditties
once left on the machine
by a voice like rum molasses.

Sex is the opiate of the masses.

Dirge and drudge. She'll hum, she'll trudge
from lunch to newshour drizzled with blood
and redundancies.

Memories splash shadows from Earth's slow curve,
run their fingers 'round the teacup's rim,
suck the gritted sugars.

The gritted teeth with which we greet
the world. The grey seep, root-deep
where all that once glittered feels old.

The vanishing point creeps ever nearer.
Her perspective: crepuscular; sneakthief;
the setting sun a blossom she can almost
reach out and pluck.

She gets her coat. The wolves have come,
the time is right for dancing.

In the East the Runners are Rising

for Paul Astorino

They are slipping from sheets, untangling from quilts. They are rousting themselves from their solitary nests or blooming from the cocoon of a lover's embrace. From Portland to Port St. Lucie, they are stumbling down hallways, lurching into walls—dreamsick, half-hungover, walking haltingly on gimpy hamstrings. Their IT bands are tight as banjo strings. Their Achilles ache. They mutter to themselves, totter toward bathrooms, peek into bedrooms where the children are singing in their sleep. They limp downstairs, slip into laundries to plunder the dryer for socks. They glance at clocks, gravitate toward kitchens where they sip their water, steep their tea, knock back a second cup of mud and await their resurrection. They tear into energy bars, butter and smash bananas onto toast, wash them down with dregs of oolong, the dank last drops of cold dark roast. The paper slaps the porch, the air fills with the roar of mowers or blowers, the clank and growl of garbage trucks. Their yearning grows as the yard dogs bark, as bees buzz and nuzzle the nectar from buds. On carpets and cement and hardwood they stand, in studios and townhomes and Tudors trussed in ivy. Feet at shoulder width, they are bending at the waist, they are twisting their hips. They are loosening tight, taut glutes, easing kinks from calves with alphabets written by ankles. Heads roll on necks, shoulders shrug, and the last of last night's cobwebs drop away like dirty shirts. In Casper and Boulder and Mendocino, they slumber still, but in the East, they lace their shoes. They leash their dogs. Their phones fill their heads with Mozart, M.I.A., Midnight Oil, or they tune in to the rush of blood, the 90-bpm rhythm of rubber on road. They dance down suburban streets, sprint past big city bodegas and small-town launderettes, leave their mark on beaches and bayside boardwalks, slip like shadows into woods that hush their footfalls with pine needles and loam. They are coming home. They are swifter now, their muscles flush with blood, bones bird-hollow, these animals wild with ancient adrenaline. They chatter like jays. They seize the streets like wolves. Sleek and dangerous, they are waking into their most perfect selves, howling up the sun as it climbs above the banks and bars, the forested hills, the silhouettes of shelter islands across the glittering bays. They are bursting from their skins, they're forgiving your sins. Their footsteps write a love letter to the world. With holy sweat, they sign their names, then race their shadows home.

My Meme

for Sandy Hook

My meme comes to you unarmed; unarmored.
My meme sports the embarrassing underwear
of the innocent. Hearts and teddy-bears
adorn my meme, which is up for pillow fights,
is a bird of a different feather. Let's fly away,
it says, let's flock together.
My meme goes outside in any kind of weather,
marries the anorak of sad happenstance
to the windproof pants of the prevailing pathologies.

My meme is a breeze.

My meme thinks it's Johnny Appleseed.
It brings a Macintosh for teacher,
plants flowers in the rubble of this silent,
smoking town. Gardens grow where angels
shake their rad, bad boogaloo, play a little hide-
and-seek, a little hokey-pokey with the living.

You put your left foot in…

My meme flings up jewels by the handful.
The air fills, quick with birdsong. Rubies, emeralds
litter the lawn like eighthnotes thunderclapped
from some sentient symphony. Child-choirs sing
today is the when we've all been waiting for.

My meme wears a pith helmet. No cute kittens
spritz my meme: gone for good, their bad-kitty
grammar. My meme is wildcat. Cheetahs sprint
the meme-veldt, the rainforests all a-pounce
with ocelots.

In my meme we can all change our spots.
We put our right heart in, take it out,
do the hokey-pokey and shake it all about.
In my meme we are all shaken.

We are all stirred.

We are a million clashing klaxons. Cacophony
of out-of-control sunbeams, we chase one-another
to the boundaries and back again, and that's okay,
because my meme's a playground,
and that's what playgrounds are for.

Real monkeys scamper the jungle-gym here.
The slide is a dopplered, happy, holler.
The air is full of birds, balls, the honks
and shattered chatter of the bejeweled always.

Tag games thrive in its hallways. My meme
is a sticker-book, a Crayola-ed, messy masterpiece.
You can stay between the lines if you want,
but my meme sprouts flowers
that haven't even been invented yet!

My meme is bloom, is blammo,
is bouquet.

My meme brings a howdy from a heaven where snack-time
is epic, and God's just a kid with a kaleidoscope.

1972

for David Bowie

Ziggy played guitar. I played in the outfield
for *Wyoming Tradesmen*. One time I threw
a kid out at home.

That whole season I never got a hit.
Bowie's a Hall-of-Famer.
I dreamed in color. Of hitting a homer.

Mars painted my telescope red. I was afraid
of spiders. I'd slick back my hair and sing
in the shower.

After games I'd get a Choco-Malt, some
Pixy Stix. Chicks dug rock stars
and Major-Leaguers.

Maybe I should take some BP before dinner.

At home I never got hit. A hick from the sticks,
I dreamed of being a pixie, a Dodger.
A thin white duke.

The Albuquerque Dukes won the PCL pennant.
Davey Lopes was no Bowie, but he had more hits.
I never swung the bat.

I gave the pitchers fits. I walked and walked
until their coaches made them plunk me.
They threw at my head and called me a pussy.

I'd steal second/third/home, then blow
them kisses. Knew it was better than swings
and misses.

I saw the ball better when I got glasses.

All the locals liked country, while I preferred glam.
All the young dudes
were busy dying in 'Nam.

Brinkley with death counts, catch with Dad after dinner.
I was out in left field most of that summer.

Oh Say Can You See? (The King of Space Disco Plays Camden Yards)

[Space Disco] tends to be spacey in a neurological rather than cosmological sense […]is engineered to mimic—or cause—the sensation of pleasurable discombobulation commonly associated with late-night dance floors. -The New Yorker

So what if I'm the King of Space Disco? I mean
what point today, rodeoing this onomatopoeia
of spangles and flash grenades, bluenotes
and crab shacks and stars?

What point roping, wrestling this Hindenburg down?
Of teaching it how to howl? Do I even have the chops
to bring the Big Bang bass drop that detonates,
heavy as Armageddon in the chest?
To make these organs vital for a change?

Dark matter streams down streets
where Black Lives smolder before dawn's early light.
This is angel-headed, this is rock and roll, is rocks
raining down: an angry fix for the squad car's red glare.
This is *rock it* science, is emcee squared,
right here, where the ballyard's gone ground zero.

So how to land this ship, say one thing true,
shake loose a tune that matters? Not Roman candle,
but smart-bomb, sonic boom to torch the ears
of twitchy young masses chanting *No More,
Baltimore*, shouting *Nevermore* in the twilight's
last screaming—risen-up, raven-headed flashmob
moving strobelit to the handcuffed hammering
of a telltale heart.

So I guess it's sample and beat, then into the street,
where spotlights pin riot gear
itching to bring down a beat of its own.
Gas-masked effigies of blood and bone, they rock
heavy metal and are dressed to kill,
hot for a night of clubbing, more than ready to dance.

for Freddie Gray

55

Winter bickers with spring today
and mudrunning through the breezy damp
I ponder the slobber and crunch
of maggots feasting upon the national heart,
while my own systolic thump, deemed good to go
for another four decades or so
keeps making its liquid trochees
behind my ribs. I feel perplexed, palindromic,
not sure if I'm coming or going,
and if one of those, then where?
I've never owned a pea coat or a house,
never held my own child to my chest,
listened to the twinned drumming
of our hearts, like tennis matches
played expertly on neighboring courts
on an afternoon everybody wants
to last forever. How is it that I still want
so much, when what I have been given
is so much more than I need? Someone tell me
how to give over to imagination the things
I will never come to know, how to survive
the wonder of stories gone untold.

In the shadow of the old stone wall
near the trailhead the year's first crocus
nudges up through a shrinking patch of snow.
Hunched between seasons under a watery sun,
their alliance is an easy one, the wind
abetting both melt and bloom, freeing
something ageless from the wet dirt
which covers my bare legs and everything.

A Field Guide to Migratory Birds

It's not easy relearning to fly. Even with running shoes
the color of fireballs and ice, it's not easy, crumpled
bufflehead, to unfold yourself from the driver's seat,
and become a bright little cloud.
It's not easy to skim the dune-encumbered shoreline
and scud untethered, lonely as a Wordsworth.
Hey, remember the daffodils? Remember playing tag
with gravity and actually believing you could win?
The breeze herds its purple wavelets across the sound.
The naked maples scrape their nails across the cosmos'
blue veneer and a crow flaps down, plucks the eye
from a possum pancaked on the center stripe.
Is one supposed to glean here something
about life's futility? Or maybe its utility.
When your brother died a piece of you shook loose,
flapped twice, spiraled the thermals
until it disappeared. Gravity said, "You're it."
Every summer the sparrows from the salt marsh rise.
Every autumn the beach rose shows you that death
is just a matter of perspective. The gulls sing,
the dunes encroach, your feet fall ever more uncertainly
upon your bike path by the sea. Still, you lace 'em up,

don't you—busted duck, bent finch, ungainly
assemblage of feathers—because the wind is up,
the game commences, and what choice is there really,
but to play? So you shrug yourself aloft,
frail wingéd-thingy, your shadow skimming
the dunetops weightless as song. The old velocity
still echoes in the hollows of your bones, the geese
point their arrows at the sun, and gravity surrenders
to the inevitability of your escape. Something
you've carried for years breaks loose and falls away.
Something wonderful comes home to roost and it's made
of hammers.

21st Century Autoimmune Blues

Even the flowers are trying to kill you.
Even the bread. Even the cells in your nails
conspire to drag your hands to your neck, enwrap
and enrapture your song-encrusted throat.
Your fingers make palpable the shadow
that seethes beyond the Earth's voracious curve,
play the blues that stipple the tender flesh.
It's a brand new year and histamines are all the rage.
Corticosteroids are the new black.
You've become allergic to yourself. It's body
vs. antibody, that same tired tango,
and it's way too late for dancing. Your twisted mister
blinks back from the bathroom mirror,
doesn't bother to floss. Your future is encrypted
in the walls of your bone-vault, you bury your feelings
but have to admit that things are getting grave.
Whispers pass over your body like hands.
The tossed postures of your everyday
play shadow puppets on the kitchen wall—Punch
and Judy headlining the Armageddon room.
So you spend what's left of your youth laughing
until you cry. Your eyes itch. It's just your body

trying to kill you to save you from yourself.
You're caught between a rock and a hardly place.
You're going to name your new band
Systemic Inflammatory Response, your first album,
What's Been Eating You Lately?
Maybe it's tick-borne. Maybe a fungus. Maybe
you're a character in a DeLillo novel. Your affliction
is *so* postmodern. You're so meta it's killing you.

The Enchantment of Blue Bamboozles

Mirage Hypothesis

The vastness here. The vague veering. Forever-
fevered; horizon skewed akimbo
at vanishing point. The road-addled meander
stunspun, stickyslow under too-blue sky—
sunstroked, blinding-bleak, barren
of cloudscuttle or bird—dome of dead echoes
that flutter   falter

fall.

The snakeskin shed. The skeletal evermore:
red, sagebrush mesa like painted-on Hollywood,
each badland shadow a gunslinger's gravesite,
every zephyr a banshee wail. In every heart
a desert, ribs robbed of hammering
long before love's last gasp.

The highway wisps up a sunstained shimmer,
holographic hovering lover—glimpsed
and ghostlit, roadkill glimmer,
the remembered come-hither
now empty-armed; a vagrant embrace. Peyoted

and blossomed, you bend a phantom limbo,
vision quested and stoked to a sad, slow burn,
singed in the grip of whispering inches,
believing in things unseen.

So go, muster your miracles from dunecrawl
majesties, slither skincracked; sidewinder yourself
into an untidy rapture, vestigial in empty air.

The Spraycan Picassos

The Spraycan Picassos lick your boxcars
with hungry tongues, tickle with plumes,
lower the boom with feathers of portent
and flame. They singe visions onto rust
and rumble: guerilla hex, metroplex
glyphed with polychrome pyrotechnics,
the time-warped metrics of a physics
too frenzied to fail. All hail
the tag! You're it, you're all that
and a bag to huff the fumes from.
The Spraycan Picassos breathe deep
from diaphragm, warble the rupture
at the heart of this war-torn town, hang
hardware-store *Guernicas* at all-night
red-light crossings, torch the still-life
galleries, append their grace-notes
to every coal train's coyoted howl: *A Love
Supreme* fifty miles from Davis, where kids
on bikes put rubber to road in a season
of clarity and distress, undress in fields of artichokes,
let their hearts just fall where they lie. You die
for lack of what is splattered there, you wear

the emperor's new armor where paintballs
whistle and thwock, pock the walls
behind the backs of the blindfolded falling.
Hear the Picassos roar! They are more
than meets the eye: Krylon commandos;
expressionistas of rap and blue guitars;
rube cubists muttering hip-hop hosannas,
hallucinogenic onto rhomboids of rolling
steel. They whisper hypnagogic, come-
hithered goodbyes, your eyes smeared
with the pigment that sets
the world on fire. You feast on figments
splashed faster than retinas can register.
Midnight's high-noon. A gunslinger moon.
The Spraycan Picassos, they kiss you
with tattletale tongues, infect you
with naphtha and hue, and you, you open
a vein. Hypnotic, narcotic, a trance
of bloodred light. Becalmed, you throb
at the crossroads: junction of midnight
and noplace—bell-rung, signal-strobed
and pulsing—while in the cities,
the Spraycan Picassos are melting
into the dawn-drowned streets like ghosts.
Heaven-spurned hosts, their prayer

flags shudder and start to roll,
their signatures still wet, charred Sharpies
still fevering their fists.

Gusher

We all leak from the same wound.
We all ooze with the same urge to drench
and dazzle and run. Only the velocities
are different, the volumes. O geyser
of sulfurous stink, I am the confetti
tossed at your pride parade! My sweetie
erodes mountains with her kiss,
the pace of her glacial love. Her trickle-down
tingles in my permafrost. I know a guy
who floods the valley every spring,
then runs back underground to play
with his ghostly fishes. Wildflowers
and rutabagas kiss in the whispers of his tread.
Uncle Lou, heralded by foghorns, says
he never meant to cause the pileup, but loves
hiding hikers in herds of deer. Waterfall,
you're a showoff, but even the suicides
adore your rain machine.
In every downpour, diamonds. In every river
a gullet full of stone. A deluge yodels
in the guts of the geode. If this is Monday
I must be a cloud; Friday, cornice flossed

from the tooth of an Alp. Look Ma,
I'm an avalanche! Is it a coincidence
that tears and amniotic fluid are chemically
so similar, or just ironic? My spirit animal
is a hailstone. Whitewater is my happy place.
Cumulonimbus, clobber me with your electric kiss.
Mountain I gushered from, guzzle me back
to your mother lode.

Ashbery Before Bedtime

so of course these dreams dash thin as whippets,
whistle candy-corn concertos: king
coyote superstars, star-speckled and howling
lunatic harmonies. Wolf-whistle-boy-howdies
and don't this bayou wear its moonbeams
coquettish: mosshung rakish interludes, angle-
art so deft at dazzlement, splashy like Pollock
like shipwreck samurai.

Swordplay on the lido-deck with Fred Astaire
overtones, Ginger-
ale and the red-heads all a-riot, their Knicks
in a twist 'cause Carmelo's getting chubby. Checker
my past in cab-ride with floozy:

To the Garden, Jeeves, and step on it!

We are stardust, we are golden. Every greenlight
gives good glint: Go-go-*a-go-go* and I drive
the lane in style: alley-ooped
and dunked in cuppa, keeping caffeinated in case
of can-can with Rockette.

Rocket man, burning out my fuse, but not alone,
my candle at both ends alight.
First fug, then wordsmithery, whiz-bang over eggs
and a bit more joe. And the sun cracking
yolks, mad over Manahatta.

Mona Lisas and Mad Hatters had for a trinket, rockets
ridden over Spanish Harlem tinseled
in drips of yellow and green.

Suddenly everything honks. It is 5:41, it's *full fathom
five,* the dog-walkers tap-dancing
the yellow brick road. It's the end of the beginning
of the outbreak of love. She whispers when

are you going to come down? Big yellow taxi
and another lad crashed on the landing,
the lone-wolf hour over and *out
damn Spot,* curled at darling's feet and sleeping.

Pan-Olympic

No one missed my shadow, not the flame,
nor the white people sparkling the lake
like reflected stars, the deck wafting cedar,
my shadow wafting back to the city,
back door open to the alley, garden hoses
and gold medals arranged like surgical
instruments, foreign words everywhere.
Is that why I fartlekked this far over
the cactus-addled rockheaps, my torso
bedecked with surprising stickers?
I had no idea. About the best-in-the-world
machine, the non-weight-bearing psyche;
the Nike campus in Beaverton, Oregon.
No idea about the survivors of the chase
patterning air: deft, anarchic pain, finish line
sundered, arms wide like Jesus, grin
a rictus of suffering—the holy kind that tastes
a little like vomit, a little like something
by Blake. How sweet to stagger, to stop,
to prostrate oneself on the logo-infested
pavement. Something wind-addled wafts
off to haunt the air above the flyover states.

My shadow, released on its own recognizance,
stitches itself back to my heel, chases me
around the track, just once, for fun.

Asian Fusion Cuisine (Or: Takeout Meets its Match in Young Jack Spratt)

> *These Chinese people sure can cook!*— (Overheard in a Thai restaurant)

At the Abe Vigoda Pagoda we feast
on sketchy fish. We douse in special sauce.

Your weight-gain's my loss; your string beans
are boss. We sprinkle
secret spices from our plot behind the house.

The waitress is a dish. The chef is a louse.

The special is octopus almandine, It screams
of David Carradine. Everybody loves our kung
fu lighting, everybody dim sum tonight.

Dessert is spring roll, caramel roll,
Jelly Roll Morton.
You can't karate chop when you're
in a full Nelson.

Bruce Lee says that I'll be hurtin' for certain
if I don't stop driving his hot-rod Lincoln.

I see Saigon, I see France, I've got a ninja
in my pants!

Sake and hockey tonight at our pad! Thai
stick, snow pea, hot wasabi. *Godzilla vs. Kimchi,*
the nuclear cabbage.
I've got the munchies, I want sausage.

Pot stickers of chicken
and dumplings of pork, *sure*, Kwai Chang's

from China, just like Robin's from Ork.

for Dan Donaghy

EDM (Ecstasy Defies Me)

Eunice in a donkey mask. Drunken monkeys on the esplanade. Dukes in epaulettes swill Maker's Mark, make a mockery of my eurotrash decorum. *Enter My Dungeon,* entreats the marquee above the door, as downstairs, DJ Machiavelli unmasks deadmau5, dons espadrilles, mixes the devil's elevator music. Diabolical elf madrigals and eventually the mind disappears. Entrails melt in the deafening muddle, drumbeaten eustaceans metastasizing: a dystopian euphony. *Electronic mind fuck,* Eunice says, *Electrogothic monkey funk.* Ecstasy denies me. Elsewhere, dentists drill to Mozart, enjoy mellow dinners, mixed drinks and the marriage bed. *Drink-up, Monkey,* Eunice says. She says *Molotov,* means *Mazel tov,* drags me onto the dancefloor. *Another mine disaster, Millie!* she cackles, *Another dose for Mommy!* Mon Dieu! More dopamine, more ephedrine for the dregs of expiring minds. Mere euthanasia for the dandied masses, candy for the dwindling middle classes. More errant dubs, more melted ears as the ermine of dark descends. Decibels escalate, Eunice masturbates deliriously. More than enough for me, my darling, my darkling dance-machine. Is there no end to this demented masquerade? Eunice, dear, your entropy defines me.

Monochrome Attic #1

(An Exhibition)*

white wedding

We loved pressed flat like flowers,
our petals crushed between covers
untitled like clouds.
We wore tinted lenses to texture
the liminal, the limnal light,
that monotone translation: invisible
painting, white wall, white noise wind-
generated and fusing field to sky

—horizonless—

white wail, refugeed trees ghosted
and fingerbranched, scrimshaw-
scratched onto retina, but Snowbaby,
tattooed with disappearing ink,
you surfed the sweetest spot,
ecstatic in x-ray specs, snowblind
on waves of silvery static.
Virginal, the history that cultivates
such a vanishing.

crimson, no clover

We sported Sherpa hats, rose-colored glasses, carried on at altitudes where the tree-smashed sky shuddered down in shards, our eyes ribboned red merely looking at the hole the sun fell through. All posy-flecked was the snowlight then, the slit wrists of ancient afternoons still bleeding out their version of events. You posed nude in fields of poppy and pomegranate: happy apple; little hymen-splash; sun that crisped my eyes to ember.

black is the new black

This loss of light—of appetite: long gone
the taste for blood, for blood orange,
for juices roaring red diatribes down chin.

With blacktooth eyes I gnaw the din
of bone-dead jitters, locked in this box
by a jailor who shares my name.

The trees have garnered a gallows glow,
here in woods where once we hung
our new skeletons out to dry.

You are still the throb, racing the crimson
capillaries of Earth's insatiable curve,
while in my blackout glasses, I am the sound

of footsteps receding, tiny echo
that throbs in Zero's empty heart.

After Yves Klein

Cabin Fever (Sculpture Garden in Security Light)

for Rebecca Gottlieb and Lina Taylor-Griggs, sculptresses of snow

Out back the snow deer's losing its head,
its sleek neck chewed away by carnivorous wind.
Branch-antlers drift a cold dust-to-dust
where trees don a Motown shuffle, glittery,
black and Orphean. The wind arranges
snowdrops and icicles by porchlight just so:
kinderkonzert; collage that kisses to obscure
—a gust and a crystal blue protrusion—
flimsy furniture and the fire-pits of fall.
The shed hides its mice behind windows
blind as the river's fishy heart.
And whence the fence, the birdbath,
the bleached bones of picnic tables and wooly
mammoths? The snow bear knows,
but keeps mum. Shadows shamble and lurk
among white obelisks with a stillness that hurtles
at sickening speed, the whole of space melting
as it freezes, spotlit pantomime of hanging
and falling forever. Icicles brush my cheek

and later I dream of daggers, of tender ventricles
pierced to gushing, of red heat Pollocked
into snow-flesh that knows how to keep a secret.

True Bride

I am colorfast. I am

blue. And who am I anyhow
without this thorninside, this drizzle of dark
chocolate where all the banjos
have run away, all the antique wedding gowns
having flown the coop,
their hangers plinking in closets
like mandolins, my girlish dreams
all fingerpicked and lightningsprung,
splattered against walls like movie screens,
like movie screams ascending
crescendos of multiplex moonlight
from a wilderness of weeds and drive-ins
where backseat beddings beget shotgun weddings.

We are gathered, and I am left
unaltared,
ungroomed in my vintage finery,
unmarried
to this notion of happy ending, free
to unspool

before the end of the reel.

So bring me a picker, my fiddlers three.
A toast to my health, then find me
a taxi a threshold I can carry myself over.
I am borrowed, and I am true.
I am fifty-foot
and flickering. I take the cake, and you

just run.

Rancid, Gladys

I am not radio friendly. I am not frequency,
I mean *frequently* tuned-in,
seldom turned on, (no hummable hooks) but still
I broadcast my etudes my little ditties,
which may someday be received
by sensitive mechanisms. Pseudopodia will tap,
antennae will wave, and thus will I be big
in Alpha Centauri the way Night Ranger is big
in Japan. If I am buttons, the zeitgeist is a zipper:
efficient, sure, but bereft of anticipatory fumbling,
no sweaty palms, her voice going
suddenly husky, and just as the tastiest sandwich
is the pilfered sandwich, the tastiest kiss
is the kiss stolen behind the drapes at the party,
lips devoured like canapés, the feasters groping
backlit unknowingly on someone's terrace
where lightning licks the last morsel of song
from the throat of the nightingale.
Is it a love song, the note stuck
behind the refrigerator magnet, the note that says
the milk is rancid, Gladys, but the raspberries
are sweet? Is it still a love song

if she leaves for the market and never comes back,
everything you ever said to her lost,
spinning off into the galactic nevermore like slang,
already out of date where syllables coalesce
into slaggy gibberish and stagger off to die
behind the fridge? Lightning licks kiss-shaped
shadows from my wall. Thunder mumbles
its incoherent odes, while the canary, bright
on her perch of flame, stands mute.
Across the alley a party flares dimly, while inside
me someone begins singing. Somewhere far away
a spaceman starts tapping his feet.

Freedom Toast

She said she was suffering from ennui I thought she said Henri so I say screw him anyway his tiny police cars funny sirens his *demitassefrissonoh-la-la*. His Napoleonic advances frozen in the Waterloo of her glare now reflected at me by a wine glass half-full which in a French accent sounds like *awful* and by the way is—this wine I mean—just as happiness sounds like *a penis* which is what Mme. Charles De Gaulle once told reporters was the most important thing one could have in this life.

In Cambridge, Maybe

The border collie hangs in low earth orbit,
plucks, then shakes the last hint
of hover from the Frisbee's tatty husk, trots back
glam-slobbery, show-off nonchalanting,
all frolicsome and furblown in the hippie wind.

University eights slice the diamondglint
of little wavelets, oars in sync—oh, rally on,
little coxswain!—while clouds like clipper ships
frisk the wind, race their regattas
on a sky so blue it sings:

O fleet figurehead, rain down your wake
of swift shadows, make the most of this major
motion picture: champagne chiaroscuro hell-bent
and heaven-sent; a fleet blight barely bleak even;
merequick ravenwing; a brushup
against the maples' mad dancing all pinky-gold.

And you, my dear! Eyes-open dreaming,
you gallop your own hundred directions:
one part headlong, kaleidoscopic stagedive,

two parts refracted light—autumnal;
loosed like broken glass, oh wow,
it's *yesterdaytomorrownextJuly,* and love,
well love bends time better than a black hole.

See: your hand
's in mine again and time is (suddenly) squishy
and way more colorful than we'd ever imagined!

Fro\m downriver a victory roar Dopplers past, a faint
splish-splash.

Gull-cry, gray from up cloudward.

From someone's window, a Chopin nocturne,
so tart at the end of apple-time, the man
with the Frisbee singing *Nearer, My Dog, to Thee.*

Aurora Borealis

Hey waiter, this isn't what I ordered! I wanted
the orgasmic happy-ever-after, side-order of sheets
smelling of sunshine and musk?

...*not* the cold can of beans no after-dinner mint,
these thunderheads to thirty thousand.

How rudely I've been treated! Turned out, tossed
scruff-and-britches onto the green-sky prairie,
saloon doors aflap, my gal ascending the backstairs
on the arm of some new buckaroo.

Cumulonimbi lightning-lasso pale cottonwoods
bent to guzzle muddy
braided rivers. O I am staggered, hailswept, tongue-
lashed and unbefriended, the stoic moo-cows
hunkered flank to wind, acting as though I'm not
even here.

Why, I oughtta....

I like old books where cows are called *beeves*.
I like menus where cows are called steak.
I like being exfoliated briskly, shower hot,
sudsy with my sweetie, hypnotic yodel
of the Raveonettes on the stereo is that
too much to ask?

Guess so…but let us stop and count we now
our blessings:

Got me still my bankroll, bedroll—my steed
my trusty steed.

Got me my yin, my yang, my bang-bang—
the enchantment of blue bamboozles.

The wind clears swiftly the sky.
Solar particles storm the stratosphere,
sing me off to that hyperborean bunkhouse
where naked cowgirls ride herd my horny dreams.

Oh Garcon, please, a nightcap! Bring me
the swift kick of whiskey, coyote narcolepsy,
my sidekick, the cloud-baffled moon.

The Razorteeth of Newsfeed

Hotel Ashbery

after John Ashbery's "Hotel Lautreamont"

1.

We arrived after eleven, yet a light burned in the window.
A storm had ransacked the woods. We became lost in the
 emerald,
the glistening, the chorus of tree frogs croaking in the gloaming,
the oratorios of coyotes and owls, which was Sibelius.

A storm had ransacked the woods. We became lost in the
 emerald.
On the wall behind the sofa a painting with boom boxes and
 tractors,
the oratorios of coyotes and owls, which was Sibelius.
The lights burned gaily, though the prayer flags murmured
 at half mast

on the wall behind the sofa: a painting with boom boxes and
 tractors.
They gave us a nightcap and a map to the station.
The lights burned gaily, though the prayer flags murmured
 at half mast:
A death in the family, we must soon be moving on.

They gave us a nightcap and a map to the station,
a flashlight, a book, the keys to a vintage Bugatti. Each
    poem tells of
a death in the family. We must soon be moving on.
The horns of elfland swing past playing dirges and Dixieland.

2.

A flashlight, a book, the keys to a vintage Bugatti. Each
    poem tells of
a minuet gone missing, a ghost in the machine, a lost ballet
    where
the horns of elfland swing past playing dirges and Dixieland.
The Spanish moss mutters of Mississippi,

a minuet gone missing, a ghost in the machine, a lost ballet
    where
the music is a kind of flagellation, an entity of sound.
The Spanish moss mutters of Mississippi
and we hover between inertia and ennui in a spectral pas de
    deux.

The music is a kind of flagellation, an entity of sound,
It plucks at our sinews like harp strings

and we hover between inertia and ennui in a spectral pas de
        deux,
Tantric on a heap of silken jammies.

It plucks at our sinews like harp strings,
this concerto for lichen and lightning bug, this pulsing
Tantric on a heap of silken jammies,
the stars rearranging themselves into more fluent constellations.

3.

This concerto for lichen and lightning bug, this pulsing
like neon in Jazztime, or a woman wriggling from a dress,
the stars rearranging themselves into more fluent constellations
of black silk, ten thousand avenues of fire.

Like neon in Jazztime, or a woman wriggling from a dress
as a train rattles the windows, and now he believes the rumors
of black silk, ten thousand avenues of fire.
Back home a teakettle whistles, breaking the survivor's reverie

as a train rattles the windows, and now he believes the rumors
scrawled on walls and derelict telephone booths.
Back home a teakettle whistles, breaking the survivor's reverie
for the last time.   He searches for clues

scrawled on walls and derelict telephone booths,
cryptic runes whispering auguries and forgotten librettos.
For the last time he searches for clues,
which as always are inscrutable as steamclouds etched on air.

4.

Cryptic runes whispering auguries and forgotten librettos
glyph the wainscoting with rumors of *Locus Solus*,
which as always are inscrutable as steamclouds etched on air.
He sighs, loses himself in records that shimmy,

glyph the wainscoting with rumors of *Locus Solus*.
We finish the poem, bittersweet as Belgian chocolate,
we sigh, lose ourselves in records that shimmy,
serenade us to sleep in this old hotel.

We finish the poem, bittersweet as Belgian chocolate.
All the old showstoppers parade so prettily,
serenade us to sleep in this old hotel.
We slip into a quieter future, turn our backs for now upon

all the old showstoppers parading so prettily.
We arrived after eleven, yet a light burned in the window.
We slip into a quieter future, turn our backs for now upon
the glistening, the chorus of tree frogs croaking in the gloaming.

Sock Hop

I came here this evening to think about fate,
but now this new frenzy of pink chiffon,
painted-blue sky, flimsy clouds of crepe paper
writhing to the whispers of unseen machinery
while electric guitars move us like marionettes
from free-throw line to tip-off circle,
convulsive as kittens biting through lamp cords
while the twins are at soccer practice.
A flux has been busted, so one hesitates to touch
them goodbye. I came here tonight to think
about how life's just a ladder leading
to another ladder, a child's game 3-D printed
and hung to span the firmament.
Or maybe a web, glistening in cosmic foreverlight,
everything lassoed to everything else.
And so we shimmy, shuddering as one
in the HVAC wind, as beautiful as we are complicit,
droplets turning to jewels in the discolight.
Inside the gymnasium the walls are mirrored,
the music a wreath of violets (I mean *violins,* I mean
violence) throbbing where our synapses used to be.
Everyone here is snazzy and aerobic,

transplanted from flash-bulbed family rooms,
spirited to this operating theater where nobody
knows how to perform the procedure.
Our fear is a single bright balloon plucked
from the breeze by filaments sticky with desire.
Someone flips a switch and the mind sings
as it burns. "Fire loves me!" we chant,
pogoing madly, our fingers wiggling at the end
of our arms like cartoon flames. We are radiant
and ephemeral. We are butterflies guttering
in the rubble. We are happy, we just don't know it yet.

Note to Self

Stay in bed.
Hide in your hoody until the sky stops
pointing its weapons at the school bus,
until *The Olivia Tremor Control* and a suitable
armor against the razorteeth of newsfeed.

Until *Neutral Milk Hotel,* Irish Breakfast
and Eggos, until you're chill, totally dope
in your new exoskeleton of leftover Legos,
Lincoln Logs, the scuffed sheen of Barbie's long,
lost limbs. Maybe then you can walk

to work without flinching at random hellos.
Maybe then you can be disarmed
by the cupcake lady, the barber, by kids
popping like corn outside the alternative arts
high school, juiced on bodega joe and Kendrick Lamar,
your own veins vibrating like banjo strings,
like you've been mainlining birdsong and twang.

If you were a superhero your special gift
would be a force-field in wildflower hues.
You'd spread petals that smell like lavender,
repel bullets and bullshit and pundits' clever talk.

Yeah, you'd spin that stuff like spidersilk,
weave an aura, an aurora, a borealis that throbs
with so much joy that even the cops get high,
the lonely boy with his bad magazine
forgetting why he came here anyway.

But all you've got is *Lunch Poems* in your pocket,
a buck ninety-eight, headful of Venn diagrams
and metaphors weaving magic against murder.
And maybe that's enough, at least for today,
because the Pride kids are selling *Krispy Kremes*
in the humanities building lobby with fabulous hair
and in your own classroom
the students are still very much alive,
even laughing at your jokes before they open
their notebooks, pull out their pages, fling poems
at the wall like spaghetti like spells for sanity,
and some of them stick.

Racial Profiling for Dummies

for Trayvon Martin

Like a cop calling the kettle,
Kanye is the new black,
but I'll stick with Prince
'cuz paisley is slimming.
My prose is purple.
Do I look phat in this?
I'm fly. On the wall. I'm
wallpaper. I see you.
"Street" is code for *Shoot*
the little bastards.
I'm street. I ride a car
named *Desire*. My hoodie
has a "Don't Walk" sign on it.
My Skittles are ammo; this tea
is *dope*. My sugar high
makes you happy for trigger.
You have me fingered.

The Lone Ranger is riding tonight.
Yippee ki-yay, motherfuckers.

The Runners in the Snow

after Bruegel's The Hunters in the Snow

Two hours in, we trudge the ridgeline, lead-legged,
faces numb, rime of breath-frost ghosting
our eyelashes, our beards, our backs bent
under the glacial weight of miles. Our skinny dogs
are weary from porpoising the drifts, chasing
the echoes of last summer's rabbits down dream-
holes in crusted snow. Above the town/below
the skim milk sky, we find ourselves pinned
to this landscape, no more free than the brush-
strokes of crows who smear themselves
across the flat, matte, hunkered-down hulk of cloud.
The afternoon wears claustrophobia like a cloak,
the chimney smoke pressed to the rooftops,
the rachitic branch-tips of trees. No velocity,
no escape. The horizon—shredded by steeples,
the broken canines of peaks—seems fixed,
phony, vanishing point the gunmetal river pours
itself into. A creeping quiescence: color-suck,
sound-suck, ice-water coalesces in our limbs
even as we drizzle ourselves over one last hilltop
between forest and home. And then a cry

like birdsong vaults from the valley, scarlet dialect
our startled blood remembers. A kid, a pond hockey
hat-trick, and afternoon's chest cracks open,
the day erupts into a whole new kind of awake. Joy
is an iceberg, but sometimes it geysers
from your heart like steam. So we haul ourselves
up onto our toes, race each other over the crest,
tumble into town in an avalanche of howls and hollers,
the ecstatic singing of dogs. This is how spring begins.

What Happens in Church

Another mudfunked Sunday, singletrack tripping
nine miles through the leafdeep and flat
fall light, not tumbling, somehow, over rocks
or roots, lungs sucking sweet oxygen
from the crystal, heart thundering red diatribes
the cardinals marry their carols to.
Your head is mostly empty, but your legs are full
of zoom, so you hurdle without thinking
the fallen body of a birch, which Saturday late
in a carnival of wind, gave up its forever bending
and finally went for broke. You have no idea
if it fell in a tirade of roots ripping, its knotted
torso torn from glacial till, or if slipping
from soil, it let go this earth with a satisfied sigh.
You know only that you'll never speak
the language of softwoods. You'll never ease
the grieving of worms. The mushrooms build
their bookshelves where birchbark used to be,
recite the natural histories with tongues

of rot and flame. Leaves float down in a ringing
of bells that only the salamanders can hear.
You pluck one from the breeze, hold it to your ear.

for Robert Wilcox, 3/9/1939-11/29/2017

On Encountering a Rack of Hogwarts Panties at Target the Husband Has an Existential Crisis

You need a pillow for the couch, a lampshade.
It's ten minutes until closing, so you take a shortcut
through the acres of undies, and both of you
are brought up short in a cartoon bazaar of cotton
and silk, startled by the plethora of underthings,
candy-colored and licensed, archipelago
of unmentionables adorned with Harley Quinn
and Spiderman, Wonder Woman, Power Rangers
and Powerpuff Girls. Hogwarts has an island
all its own: hangers slung with the come-hither
of Slytherin boy-briefs: black, trimmed in green
and mockery. Crimson and gold Gryffindor hipsters
hang all holier-than-thou, and buddy,
you can rest assured you will never be smart enough,
brave enough, *wizard enough* to fathom whatever
magic they might conceal. Nor young enough.
No, never again, and you can feel your face redden
as you turn away from the rack from which bikinis
dangle, bedecked with the Hogwarts crest: navy
with maroon, or maroon with navy, depending,

you tell your love, upon whether the games
are home or away. You both chuckle in your middle-
aged underclothes, but you sense the flickering
of long-ago flames. They flare, unbidden,
flashing their ironic Underoos from candlelit rooms
of yesteryear, a little bit drunk, cracking jokes
about spells and magic wands until your love says,
Honey, you're sweating. Are you okay?
Moments later, safe among the throw-pillows,
your faces lit by a hundred flashing televisions,
it hits you: the perfection of Deadpool boxers
and Captain America briefs, of Wonder Woman
bloomers like magic lassos for the libidos
of the unsuspecting, undergarments
exactly as glorious, as ludicrous as the genitals
they are woven to conceal. And then
it's the witching hour. You are instructed to bring
all items to the register, so having decided
on the purple pillow with polka-dots, you begin
to make your way to the front of the store.
But in the aisle between men's accessories
and lingerie you stop. Casually, you pluck a pair
of Harry Potter boxers from the rack, drop them
into your cart. Your love cackles, grabs a pair
of *homes*, a pair of *aways*. You howl low,

like a wolf, and on the wall the big-screen TVs seem to have changed channels all by themselves. Every last one wears the face of Nina Simone, and she's singing *I Put a Spell on You.*

Live Model at the Salon for Abject Expressionists

an auto-cento for Joan Mitchell

Painters in Nirvana T-shirts shout color at canvas,
keep their eyes peeled for the future writhing
in clots of viscous smoke. They swag tradeshow
totebags. They polish their pistols in your blood,
whistle through badlands of slag and ash, flash
their Underoos, blackout drunk and cracking wise
about shotgun weddings or pigment that'll set
your hair on fire. The river rages with snowmelt.
Remember when silver hammers knocked you
in the knees among summer's tender tufts?
Here, even the flowers are trying to kill you.
Somebody says a blessing over the tater tots.
Your head is white noise, but your footprints litter
the lawn like eighth-notes thunderclapped
from some sentient symphony. You're a valentine
with a switchblade inside, geyser of figments
splashed faster than retinas can register. Red,
red pickup truck. Stubblefield crusted with snow.
Hey, maybe you should shatter yourself, seduce
them into swallowing shards. Mayhap you should

hang a mosaic of baby pics and dropped crockery,
murder your crows in a burst of blood
and feathers, conjure an onomatopoeia of spangles
and flash grenades, bluenotes and crab shacks
and stars. You can't sit still, so you gallop
a hundred different directions, one part pink
ladyslipper, two parts bullet in cahoots with the sky.
Not sin, but satisfaction at first light.
The gods be in your head, your brush ablaze.
Your name? *It doesn't matter.*

Nude Descending a Staircase

Moonstoned in the depths of the *Ambien* hours,
she flows, bedroom to kitchen to bath, naked,
gravity-lover downstairs dancing,
unembarrassed as whitewater in a kayaker's dream.

Sleek and dangerous, she hypnotizes: my Salome,
my mistress of hydrodynamics and dance.
Swamped in veils, in waves in brush strokes,
what can I do but founder: twee playboat
capsized in her aftermath, shouting out, *not waving,
but drowning!*

O shapeshifter, sharpshooting mad under moon,
descend untouched, untouchable, slip aqueous
through my luckless grasp—*liquidshimmery, lickety-
split*—reflections tonguing lovers lost in new ideas
of what is face, what is form where current is king.

No mudpuddle Narcissus, I only have eyes
for the rushing by, the burning too quick
for retina to register, for beauty in fleetest form
setting the ruined millworks afire

out beyond the rainglossed highway,
where muscle cars whoosh puddles into oilslicked
masterpieces, streetlit abstract expressions:
four hundred horses of paintbrush, one hundred
thousand Duchamps dancing on the head of a pin.

Ah, the hunger in your eyes, the shiny fish
writhing under your skin!
Shiver me your undulation, modulation,
your ballet, your hipsway, your come-thee-hither
from upstairs down.
For you I breathe deep, dive deep
into your sizzle and froth, scream you a song
you carry only to lose to a bigger river.
Another voice in the drowned-boy chorus,
another lullaby gone home to sleep in the sea.

Carbon Taxing

We harvest coal under a werewolf moon,
keep our eyes peeled for lumps, blacker
than panther on black. Sometimes
we pick poisonous mushrooms by mistake.
We carry bookstore totebags with pictures
of famous authors on them. Mine
has Virginia Woolf and Larry Flynt. Woolf
has a moustache made of coal dust.
She looks like a werewoolf, like Ulysses
S. Grant. Wait, that *is* Ulysses S. Grant!
It's Walt Whitman? My bad. The mushrooms
burn like damp turds. Dreams of dead animals
swirl in the smoke. On a clear day you can see,
maybe a mile. New coal ripens in the heat.
My bag is fat with lumps. The night is still.
90-proof moon, but no shine. Mountaintop?
What mountaintop?

God Particle

for GMH, wherever you are

Gravity is unaccounted for. This floating
makes a dervish of the piecemeal,
a spinning in the innards
where once a compass spun true.

Give North its due: polestar-hung horizons,
the enticements of gallows, the longquick

drop:
foreverbound, astounded, your eyes hooded
and glassed telescopic,
galaxies whirling within and without,
now such distinctions have lost all meaning.

Rhythm is sprung.
Everybody Wang Chung tonight, our quarks
configured all fairylight, like Vegas, our bearings
pulsared and nonplussed—unminused,
casinos collapsed, synapses starhung
with wreckage from the first, the last, Big Bang.

Bumper-car particles collide underfrance,
song-and-dance accelerated ungodly fast.
New universes flicker to festoon, new equations
recite the lyric of everything, forever:
Demon-lover, Windhover shadowing angelic odes…

…AND *the fire that breaks from thee then,*
a billion Times told lovelier, more dangerous.
O Fleet Falcon skylarking: skylark, hail to thee!
O alchemy, you have forged the golden key:
found-foundry, God's grandeur in workshops silent
abuzz, sub-atoms joyriding unto crash,
man-made multiverse, new verse sprung
from very nearly naught, where equations are metaphors
and everything's real.

String-theory troubadours pluck instruments fine-tuned
to figure, heavenlight dapples magnetic fields,
forever fleeting, underground, where Fury shrieks,
No lingering!

Flotsam

(In memory of America)

We find ourselves where the waves drag bodies
onto the beach. Our fingers rake the sand,
our breath salts the air, shells and seaweed spill
from our pockets like strange currencies.

Out there somewhere float rafts of plastic
twice as big as Texas, vast armadas of junk,
the guts of every fish filled with bottle-bits,
dregs of jugs, those exfoliating microbeads
delivered by the riverful to the sea.

But our skin was so soft and flushed from sun!
Our supple lips leapt like trout to catch
the wayward kisses, our every atom doing
the dance of *yes*. So *of course* we ignored
the waves with their whispered auguries.
Of course we mocked their thunder. We read
only maps that warned us not of monsters,

made gaudy landmarks of ourselves way out
in the middle of the ocean.

Oh we danced a loose-limbed conga once,
combed the swells for sprigs and frigates,
listened for intercontinental missives spilled
from the mouths of birds. The waves
devoured our footprints. We just made more.
We never once stopped laughing.
We never knew what hit us.

Coda: The Murder in Her He(art)

The Murder in her He(art)

Last thoughts: the
godhead is a fist of light
a pistol and a pestilence my maker
my destroyer I guess I always knew.
I knew names, dates
(and she couldn't have that.)

I knew the paintbrush
was trying to tell me something:
the hum and the buggery,
a thug with some sluggery.
Maybe it was something
more funny ironic than funny ha-ha

(a smattering of bandicoots)
(a splattering of pigment)
(a fidgety figment)

The city sleeps and the trees sing
ding-dong the muse is dead,
the doorstep wolves aslumber,

sated on the lawn:
one red shoe, a dandelion a sonnet
or two,

the shadetree shadow-hung,
the anklebone picked clean.

About the Author

Brent Terry has been an elementary school teacher, coach, running store manager and semi-elite runner. His poetry has won several awards and his poems, stories, reviews and journalism have appeared in many periodicals. He is the author of three collections of poetry and hundreds of unused band names. He has more pairs of running shoes than small beaches have grains of sand, and his love of Dr. Pepper is legendary. Terry lives in Connecticut, where he teaches creative writing and literature at Eastern Connecticut State University.

About the Press

Unsolicited Press is a small publisher in Portland, Oregon. The team is made up of incredible volunteers that seek to produce the highest quality poetry, fiction, and nonfiction. Follow the press on Twitter (@unsolicitedP), Instagram (@unsolicitedpress). Learn more at unsolicitedpress.com

www.ingramcontent.com/pod-product-compliance
Lightning Source LLC
Chambersburg PA
CBHW022009120526
44592CB00034B/756